Copyright © 2011 XAMonline, Inc.
All rights reserved. No part of the material protected by this copyright notice may be reproduced or utilized in any form or by any means, electronic or mechanical, including photocopying, recording or by any information storage and retrievable system, without written permission from the copyright holder.

To obtain permission(s) to use the material from this work for any purpose including workshops or seminars, please submit a written request to:

XAMonline, Inc.
25 First Street, Suite 106
Cambridge, MA 02141
Toll Free: 1-800-509-4128
Email: info@xamonline.com
Web: www.xamonline.com
Fax: 1-617-583-5552

Library of Congress Cataloging-in-Publication Data

Wynne, Sharon A.
    ILTS Assessment of Professional Teaching Tests 101-104 Practice Test 2:
    Teacher Certification / Sharon A. Wynne. -1st ed.
    ISBN: 978-1-60787-198-9
    1. ILTS Assessment of Professional Teaching Tests 101-104 Practice Test 2
    2. Study Guides   3. ILTS   4. Teachers' Certification & Licensure
    5. Careers

Disclaimer:
The opinions expressed in this publication are the sole works of XAMonline and were created independently from the National Education Association, Educational Testing Service, or any State Department of Education, National Evaluation Systems or other testing affiliates.

Between the time of publication and printing, state specific standards as well as testing formats and website information may change that is not included in part or in whole within this product. Sample test questions are developed by XAMonline and reflect similar content as on real tests; however, they are not former tests. XAMonline assembles content that aligns with state standards but makes no claims nor guarantees teacher candidates a passing score. Numerical scores are determined by testing companies such as NES or ETS and then are compared with individual state standards. A passing score varies from state to state.

Printed in the United States of America   œ-1
ILTS Assessment of Professional Teaching Tests 101-104 Practice Test 2
ISBN: 978-1-60787-198-9

Assessment of Professional Teaching Tests 101-104 Post Test

1. Brian is completing an assignment in which he was asked to solve this problem: "Matthew is to the left of Joe, and Joe is to the left of Garrett. Where is Matthew in relationship to Garrett?" Based on this type of cognitive problem, how old is Brian likely to be?

   A. Age 6
   B. Age 8
   C. Age 10
   D. Age 12

2. Lack of concentration and agitation are common signs of:

   A. Drug use
   B. Abuse
   C. Lack of nutrition/sleep
   D. All of the above

3. Which of the following statements is true concerning the ways multiple domains of development relate to each other?

   A. Physical and cognitive development impact one another the most
   B. Emotional development is the underlying basis to other areas of development
   C. Physical, social, emotional and cognitive development all impact each other
   D. Each area of development develops in a sequence, one after the other

4. Mr. Jones has a student demonstrating emotional difficulties. As a result, the student's focus and quality of work has been compromised. What is the first thing Mr. Jones should do regarding this student?

   A. Talk to the student
   B. Talk to the parents
   C. Implement strategies to help the student
   D. Talk to the special education department and/or school psychologist

5. Which of the following statements is NOT true about play?

   A. Play helps develop motor skills
   B. Play starts off cooperative and becomes more solitary as children grow
   C. Play helps children learn about themselves and their interests
   D. Sports is an appropriate type of play for some, but not all, children

6. Which of the following ways can a teacher implement to convey high expectations to students?

   A. Communicate effectively with students and parents
   B. Dilute instruction to challenged students so they can experience success
   C. Speak to the students about your confidence in their ability to succeed
   D. Notify students of your expectations first and foremost

7. **Some examples of impediments students face when developing decision-making skills include:**

   A. Inability to estimate negative consequences
   B. Succumbing to emotion over logic
   C. Inability to judge the reactions of their peers
   D. All of the above

8. **Research has shown that the organization of middle-level education is unique and important to adolescent learning because:**

   A. It is a less personal environment than elementary school
   B. It engages in content area instruction
   C. The programs are not too exploratory
   D. Varied learning strategies accommodate curiosity and exploration

9. **A positive _____ involves self-acceptance as a person, and does not imply feelings of superiority or perfection.**

   A. self-image
   B. sense of confidence
   C. self-concept
   D. self-awareness

10. **Which of the following statements has been found to be true regarding students engaging in risky behaviors?**

    A. Engaging in risky behaviors often negatively impacts learning and development
    B. Anti-social behavior is a late sign that students are engaging in risky behavior.
    C. Adolescents' limited decision-making skills are not a factor relating to risky behaviors.
    D. Emotionally healthy students have a difficult time maintain control over their involvement in risky behaviors.

11. **Which of the following statements does NOT demonstrate a teacher showing respect for the diversity of students in her classroom?**

    A. The teacher refrains from calling on reluctant students, forcing them to participate
    B. The teacher meets with students individually so as to learn about specifics such as the student's interests or to learn how the student likes to be addressed
    C. The teacher allows students to volunteer thoughts, opinions and ideas
    D. The teacher makes cultural connections that are relevant to instruction

12. James has an assignment to interview an adult from another country. For his assignment, he is to conduct a short interview and view an authentic letter or journal of the adult. He is to compile everything into a wall display with information on the country as well. This assignment is an example of:

    A. a Social Science unit
    B. inclusion
    C. establishing a culturally-rich environment
    D. an ELL assignment

13. Journals, reflections, exhibits, oral presentations, and portfolios are just some examples of _____.

    A. Cooperative learning
    B. Personalized learning communities
    C. Alternative assessments
    D. Differentiated instruction

14. Which of the following is NOT considered to be a difference in student learning ability?

    A. Giftedness
    B. Cerebral palsy
    C. Auditory processing disorder
    D. Dyslexia

15. When planning lessons and units for classroom instruction, teachers must target observable and measurable _____ in their lessons and units.

    A. objectives
    B. themes
    C. goals
    D. assessments

16. At the start of Mrs. McDonald's daily grammar lesson, she wrote "Students will learn to contrast adjectives and adverbs in written sentences" on the board for her students. This is an example of:

    A. a clear objective
    B. an unclear objective
    C. a clear goal
    D. a unit introduction

17. When evaluating one's effectiveness as a teacher, it is important for the individual to:

    A. reflect on their own teachings, as well as those of others, to determine if needs are being met.
    B. finish their education so they know how and what to teach
    C. teach their lessons over and over again
    D. come to terms with the fact that some students may never understand a specific concept.

18. Which of the following describes a common issue with the sole use of textbooks for instruction?

    A. Textbooks are suitable and age-appropriate
    B. Textbooks may reflect a single perspective or outdated societal values
    C. Textbooks provide detailed units with specific teaching procedures
    D. Textbooks follow the design and focus of the school administration

19. According to the scope and sequences of most curriculum units/plans, _____ must be taken into consideration to determine quantifiably that student learning has taken place over the course of the unit.

    A. National and state standards
    B. learning objectives, goals, and assessments
    C. learning experiences
    D. All of the above

20. Taking attendance, gathering homework, "quiet study time", and assembling members for group work are all examples of _____.

    A. a typical elementary classroom morning
    B. unavoidable teacher "chores"
    C. nonproductive time
    D. All of the above

21. _____ deal(s) with the study of how to help the learner gain understanding about how knowledge is constructed, as well as how to consciously constructed knowledge.

    A. The metacognition learning theory
    B. Piaget's stages of development
    C. The brain-based learning theory
    D. The multiple intelligences theory

22. Mr. Sillars considers his students' social needs, as well as his curriculum, when designing and implementing his classroom management strategies. By doing so, he is utilizing the _____ learning theory to enhance student learning.

    A. brain-based
    B. cognitive
    C. constructivist
    D. behaviorism

23. Bloom's Taxonomy refers to:

    A. only higher-ordered thinking skills
    B. advanced communication skills
    C. multiple levels within the cognitive domain
    D. All of the above

24. Which of the following statements is NOT true about effective questioning?

    A. Ask questions that require substantive answers
    B. Include questions with simple fact answers
    C. Don't confuse students with questions that pose contradictions to the topic
    D. Ask questions about current and real-life situations

25. Requiring students to keep assignment calendars helps students by teaching them to:

    A. keep materials organized in the classroom
    B. estimate the time needed for assignments and track due dates
    C. divide responsibilities amongst classmates and assignments
    D. practice leadership roles

26. Teaching students the use of _____ demonstrates an effective study skill that emphasizes the use of webs, maps and outlines to organize and relate material around a study topic.

    A. summarizing
    B. graphic organizers
    C. note-taking
    D. All of the above

27. Socioeconomic status, family education, crisis factors, and stated teacher expectations are all examples of factors that:

    A. decrease achievement
    B. affect education
    C. increase learning
    D. Answers B and C

28. Which of the following terms describes the state of learning in which students and teachers focus on positive reinforcement, self-management, and monitoring of progress?

    A. Initial acquisition
    B. Advanced acquisition
    C. Maintenance
    D. Proficiency

29. Megan's teacher has differentiated her art research project to include a section on demonstrating Impressionist brush techniques. By doing so, Megan's teacher has incorporated her _____ approach to learning in her assignment.

    A. Visual
    B. Auditory
    C. Kinesthetic
    D. Naturalistic

30. Mrs. Anderson engages her middle schoolers in peer review sessions, discussion journaling, and small-group learning. This classroom management style reflects Mrs. Anderson's knowledge that she:

    A. is aware of her students' developmental needs
    B. doesn't want to lecture all day long
    C. plans in-depth and complex activities for her class
    D. All of the above

31. In order to establish a classroom that encourages collaborative, respectful and supportive interactions among students, teachers must NOT:

    A. encourage the extensive participation from all students
    B. model how to welcome and consider all points of view
    C. positively affirm all student ideas
    D. deter ideas that are amiss from the topic

32. Which of the following statements is NOT an important strategy when it comes to running an organized classroom geared for optimal learning?

    A. Having prepared and ample materials for each lesson
    B. Allowing students to return materials poorly
    C. Having in-place procedures for distributing materials
    D. Having classroom management policies in place

33. **Mrs. Doyle is a new teacher who has realized it is taking a long time to get her class situated in the morning. Which of the following strategies would help her save time?**

    A. Calling out roll each morning while marking present and absent students
    B. Searching through all materials each morning before starting each activity
    C. Having each student come up to show completed homework assignments each class
    D. Laminating a class seating chart to mark empty desks for roll and to reuse each day

34. **Which of the following statements describes the small group socialization entitled "trading cards"?**

    A. Children build towers with a deck of card, working together
    B. Children share information about themselves on self-made trading cards
    C. Children move math cards to "find" the right answer in a timed activity
    D. Children create small-group stories to laminate on cards

35. **Which of the following terms describes the element of cooperative learning that states that all team members' unique contributions are required for success?**

    A. Small group skills
    B. Positive Interdependence
    C. Face-to-Face Interaction
    D. Group Processing

36. **Which of the following is NOT a common critique of block or modular scheduling?**

    A. Long instructional blocks are difficult for younger or less mature children
    B. Students can be negatively affected much if they miss a day of school
    C. Teachers are always able to plan what they want to cover in the large block
    D. It is difficult for teachers to cover ample material in advanced classes

37. **Using the available _____ to perform administrative tasks is increasingly becoming a necessity for the modern teacher.**

    A. technology
    B. curriculum
    C. standards
    D. materials

38. **Volunteers, when used appropriately, can enhance a classroom setting by:**

    A. offering assistance to just a few students
    B. relieving the teacher of some teaching responsibility
    C. providing individualized attention to students
    D. helping to plan lessons and activities

39. **This behavior management technique refers to the concept that a preferred behavior that frequently occurs can be used to increase a less preferred behavior with a low rate of occurrence.**

    A. token economy
    B. contingency contract
    C. prompting
    D. modeling

40. Common examples that would BEST describe the age-appropriate and high behavior expectations in an upper elementary or middle school classroom include:

    A. raising your hand to speak; not physical or verbal disruptions; and speaking and behaving in an age-appropriate manner
    B. keeping hands to oneself; show respect to others; and listen carefully
    C. no cheating or plagiarizing; no obscene language; no inappropriate displays of affection; and no electronic devices in the classroom
    D. clean up your area; share with others; and take turns with classmates

41. What is the estimated number of rules a classroom teacher should create with her students and display in the classroom?

    A. 1-2
    B. 2-3
    C. 4-6
    D. 7-8

42. Robert, an 11-yr-old is Mrs. Robbins' fifth grade class, is repeatedly leaving his seat during his teacher's lessons. Which of the following strategies is NOT recommended in helping Robert to modify his negative behavior?

    A. making a clear and concise statement about expected behavior
    B. making a harsh and loud statement to get a point across
    C. referring to the posted classroom rules
    D. swiftly addressing Robert's disregard for the rules as soon as he leaves his seat or even as early as when the teacher sees him begin to stand

43. Much valuable information occurs in communications which occur between teacher and student. Which of the following is a significant factor that teachers must consider when assessing student learning?

    A. A noisy air conditioner
    B. A learning disability
    C. Level of required teacher assistance
    D. All of the above

44. Mrs. Allen is conducting a discussion on the three types of rock with her fifth grade science class. As she asks the students to provide an example of an igneous rock, Jason raises his hand to go to the rest room. Mrs. Allen nods yes while repeating her question. What is this an example of?

    A. redirecting the discussion to maintain learning flow
    B. an insincere response
    C. an unavoidable class disruption
    D. a housekeeping task

45. Some teachers choose not to simply correct their students during a discussion. Instead, they choose methods, such as discussing or amplifying the response, in order to _____.

    A. waste classroom time by repeating the answers
    B. isolate students in the discussion
    C. provide no feedback
    D. show that student responses are accepted and valuable

46. Inductive reasoning:

    A. draws conclusions from finite examples
    B. considers simple facts or statements to arrive at more general conclusion
    C. theories based on assumed observations that contain at least one prediction
    D. arrives at an explanatory hypothesis

47. Brainstorming, discussions, problem solving, dramatizations, and learning centers are all good examples of:

    A. varying instructional strategies
    B. higher-ordered thinking skills
    C. inquiry
    D. cooperative learning

48. Why are teacher observations critical to the structure, pacing and effectiveness of a lesson?

    A. teachers are able to assess the needs of the students
    B. observations help to drive the lesson
    C. teachers can adjust instructional strategies as needed
    D. All of the above

49. Which of the following strategies is NOT a method teachers can use to increase motivation in their classrooms?

    A. Ask thought-provoking questions
    B. Find connections between material and student experiences
    C. Utilize charts, games or manipulatives to explore topics
    D. Use direct instruction to increase recall and boost confidence

50. When evaluating learning materials for a classroom, which of the following questions is LEAST important in that consideration?

    A. Will this material promote retention?
    B. Will this subject interest my students?
    C. Does this material promote interdisciplinary learning?
    D. Are these activities hands on?

51. _____ motivation is motivation that comes from the expectation of rewards or punishments.

    A. Intrinsic
    B. Fear
    C. Extrinsic
    D. Self-

52. What is a downfall in using punishment (or the aim to avoid such punishment) as a motivator?

    A. Students become viewed as unfair and unorganized
    B. Students eventually do not fear the teacher anymore
    C. Students become too consumed with fear they can't focus on learning
    D. Students fail to retain information as well.

53. When considering student motivation, learning and on-task behavior, research suggests teamwork and cooperative learning activities _____ student behavior problems.

    A. increase
    B. decrease
    C. don't affect
    D. eliminate

54. Having students create daily lists and/or unit goals is a strategy that helps to:

    A. create seatwork for students
    B. assess daily learning
    C. increase student motivation
    D. All of the above

55. Many school computers have strict space limitations, so when teachers cannot store files on the hard drive, another option is to store large files on portable or external _____, such as a flash drive.

    A. storage devices
    B. wiring systems
    C. computers
    D. Answers A and B

56. Which of the following is the likely type of network to be found in a school building?

    A. wide-area network
    B. local-area network
    C. campus-area network
    D. home-area network

57. What is the suggested consequence for a student who abuses or violates any parts of his or her district's computer usage agreement?

    A. three days detention
    B. provide student and his or her parent with a written warning
    C. have all access to school computers or educational technology blocked
    D. have an aid supervise the student's computer usage

58. Of what important fact should teachers make older students aware prior to students' usage of Internet resources for a school assignment?

    A. accurate information is hard to find on the Internet
    B. material on the Internet may or may not have been approved for accurate content before publication
    C. only pre-selected sites can be used
    D. it is impossible to verify validity on Internet sites

59. Which of the following is NOT a primary category of how technological tools can be used in a school?

    A. instructional/practice/assessment
    B. classroom management
    C. research
    D. creation

60. **This category of technological instructional tools refers to where students use word processing, spreadsheets, graphic, or multi-media tools to demonstrate proficiency with both the lesson knowledge and the technology.**

    A. instructional/practice/assessment
    B. classroom management
    C. research
    D. creation

61. **Mr. Jacobs utilizes a web page to list his class assignments, homework, upcoming tests and other relevant important dates. What is one or Mr. Jacobs' reasons for presenting information about his class work online?**

    A. more easily communicate with parents
    B. presents his class work in a professional and organized manner
    C. gain professional respect from parents, colleagues and administrators
    D. All of the above

62. **What is one benefit from allowing students to collaborate when working on computer programs in the classroom?**

    A. more easily communicate with parents
    B. students can work with their friends to get their work completed
    C. collaboration on computers will help student engage in a more productive, help-centered learning environment
    D. All of the above

63. **When a teacher asks student to produce a technological product, the teacher must consider several elements in their final product. When the teacher considers the *relevance* of a final product, he or she is considering:**

    A. the method of technology used
    B. to whom the product is directed and what is needed to be comprehended
    C. how the product was used to prove proficiency of the content
    D. the format of the piece

64. **This kind of assessment is a structured, infrequent measure of learner achievement.**

    A. Journal
    B. Informal
    C. Formal
    D. Observation

65. **Multiple choice tests are an example of:**

    A. Subjective assessment
    B. Objective assessment
    C. Informal assessment
    D. Authentic assessment

66. **What is one disadvantage to formal assessment?**

    A. Multiple-choice tests are too easy
    B. These assessments don't always measure specific retention
    C. These assessments don't always measure achievement
    D. These assessments don't always provide a complete picture of a student's ability

67. **Mrs. O'Neill is recording through codes the performance of her students while reading aloud. This coding is an example of an informal assessment called a(n):**

    A. observation
    B. running record
    C. journal
    D. essay

68. **Researchers suggest that a benefit of a true/false test item is:**

    A. susceptibility to guessing
    B. the questions are difficult to construct
    C. there are limited learning outcomes it can measure
    D. is useful in identifying cause and effect relationships

69. **Mr. Rockford is mentoring a new teacher, Mr. Harsche. Mr. Rockford has noticed that Mr. Harsche's comments on the students' English essays are too vague with comments such as "Work on grammar." Which of the following comments could Mr. Rockford suggest to Mr. Harsche in order for him to better provide more useful feedback to his students?**

    A. "This should be clearer."
    B. "Review last week's grammar lesson to improve."
    C. "See me."
    D. "Be sure to always use a comma to separate independent clauses in the same sentence."

70. **Benjamin is a student in Mr. Turner's American History class. He has asked a question that is slightly off topic from the lesson, but initiated by the lesson content, and it has sparked the interest of his classmates. What is the ideal thing for Mr. Turner to do at that moment in class?**

    A. have Benjamin conduct independent research on the topic
    B. move forward and ignore the question
    C. respond to this "teachable moment" and adjust the class discussion
    D. re-teach the original concept so as to get the class back on task

71. **What is one benefit of a teacher using an online web site or classroom management system?**

    A. Attendance can be tracked
    B. Class assignments, tests and due dates can be viewed anytime
    C. Parents can communicate almost directly with the teacher at their convenience
    D. All of the above

72. **Mrs. Gains wishes to better communicate with her students' parents on a more regular basis. What is a strategy Mrs. Gains can implement in order to achieve improved communication?**

    A. Create a class newsletter
    B. Call home regarding negative behavior
    C. Send a note home once a year
    D. Meeting at conferences is sufficient

73. Three of the following four statements suggest ways for teachers to work with diverse groups in the classroom. Which statement is NOT a suggested way to encourage positivity in diverse classrooms?

    A. show respect to all parents, students and families
    B. disregard negative actions from difficult families
    C. talk personally with each student
    D. emphasize partnerships with students to enhance their education and development

74. Which of the following is NOT a purpose of a parent-teacher conference?

    A. to obtain information about the child
    B. share information with the parents about the performance and behavior of the child
    C. socialize with the teacher to catch up on school events
    D. request parental support or involvement in specific activities

75. _____ can supplement the minimized and marginal educational resources of school communities.

    A. Advanced curriculum materials
    B. Community resources
    C. Parents
    D. Administrators

76. According to some researchers, connections between the school and the community encourage:

    A. a commitment to volunteering
    B. a sense of community and value
    C. greater retention rates of graduating students
    D. All of the above

77. Team teaching consists of:

    A. mentoring systems
    B. two or more teachers involved in the same classroom instruction
    C. one grade level of teachers integrating subjects across the grade and then teaching one of those subjects to all grade classes
    D. groups of educators of the same discipline (but for different levels) working to plan curriculum

78. This educational professional serves as the leader in the development and implementation of a subject.

    A. technology coordinator
    B. child study team
    C. curriculum coordinator
    D. subject administrator

79. How can teachers utilize resources outside the school to enhance professional development?

    A. research and make use of state initiatives
    B. utilize training and workshops provided by service centers
    C. work with universities to test new strategies and activities
    D. All of the above

80. What is the typical first step for a principal conducting a teacher appraisal to take?

    A. evaluate and establish the goals and objectives teachers will work to attain
    B. provide recommendations for professional development
    C. encourage the teacher to seek out support from other teachers and/or mentor
    D. alleviate the teacher's concern

81. Which of the following is a constructive outcome of teacher self-assessment and self-reflection?

    A. the teacher can identify what areas they should not teach
    B. the teacher can contribute information to academic trends
    C. the teacher realizes which upcoming staff development opportunities are futile
    D. the teacher comes to identify areas of skill that require improvement

82. Which of the following educational professionals is NOT typically part of a Child Study/Core Team?

    A. special education teacher
    B. school psychologist
    C. guidance counselor
    D. curriculum coordinator

83. Mr. Jackral suspects Jeremy, one his students, is being physically abused. What should be Mr. Jackral's initial step?

    A. wait to affirm the abuse
    B. talk to the student's parents
    C. talk to administration immediately
    D. talk to a colleague and think it over before acting

84. Ms. Allen, the school Media Specialist, has seen a new teacher, Ms. Bellamy copying a chapter of a children's literature novel for use in her classroom. Should Ms. Allen approach Ms. Bellamy to discuss copyright infringement according to the "Guidelines for Classroom Copying in Nonprofit Educational Institutions"?

    A. yes; a chapter of prose exceeds the guidelines
    B. no; no copyright infringement has occurred
    C. no; a chapter of prose is acceptable by the guidelines
    D. yes; no copying of books is allowed

85. A common pressure for new teachers is:

    A. the intense rules and regulations regarding behavioral management and professionalism
    B. likelihood of abuse violations
    C. maintaining a toolkit of instructional strategies
    D. All of the above

86. Which of the following pieces of information is NOT required to be compiled in a student's permanent file?

    A. medical and physical information
    B. educational assessments, attendance and anecdotes
    C. social interests
    D. personal information

87. **The contents of a students' permanent record:**

    A. should be indicative of student aptitude
    B. are highly confidential
    C. should be constructive and presented positively
    D. All of the above

88. **Reliability of an academic assessment refers to:**

    A. the extent that assessments are consistent over time and setting
    B. the appropriateness of the test scores
    C. the ease of the procedures of the test
    D. the accessibility of academic information on the test

89. **Some of the primary responsibilities of _____ include monitoring operations of schools, hiring teachers, managing bus and food services.**

    A. a school district
    B. a local state service center
    C. a state government
    D. the US Department of Education

90. **It is crucial that teacher maintain the highest of professional standards. In order to do so, teachers must:**

    A. collaborate with peers professionally
    B. continue their own professional development with higher education and professional organizations
    C. utilize state and community resources
    D. All of the above

Assessment of Professional Teaching Tests 101-104 Rationales

1. Brian is completing an assignment in which he was asked to solve this problem: "Matthew is to the left of Joe, and Joe is to the left of Garrett. Where is Matthew in relationship to Garrett?" Based on this type of cognitive problem, how old is Brian likely to be?

    A. Age 6
    B. Age 8
    C. Age 10
    D. Age 12

Answer: D. Age 12.
This problem asks Brian to reason a hypothetical problem using deductive reasoning and is an example of formal operation thought. Formal operations begin around age 11 when students can begin to develop hypotheses or best guesses, and systematically deduce, or conclude, which is the best path to follow in solving the problem.

2. Lack of concentration and agitation are common signs of:

    A. Drug use
    B. Abuse
    C. Lack of nutrition/sleep
    D. All of the above

Answer: D. All of the above.
Answers A, B, and C all share the common signs of lack of concentration and agitation. Problems in school can begin with lack of sleep and nutrition, so it is important for all students to have breakfast and get plenty of rest. In more troubled cases, teachers may observe an unfocused/agitation child and feel it is more than just lack of sleep or food. Teachers must familiarize themselves with the common signs of abuse, drug use and malnutrition so as to best help and report incidents of such.

3. Which of the following statements is true concerning the ways multiple domains of development relate to each other?

    A. Physical and cognitive development impact one another the most
    B. Emotional development is the underlying basis to other areas of development
    C. Physical, social, emotional and cognitive development all impact each other
    D. Each area of development develops in a sequence, one after the other

Answer: C. Physical, social, emotional and cognitive development all impact each other
Each element of development impacts other elements of development. All domains of development (physical, social, and academic) are integrated, and development in each dimension is influenced by the others.

4. **Mr. Jones has a student demonstrating emotional difficulties. As a result, the student's focus and quality of work has been compromised. What is the first thing Mr. Jones should do regarding this student?**

   A. Talk to the student
   B. Talk to the parents
   C. Implement strategies to help the student
   D. Talk to the special education department and/or school psychologist

Answer: D. Talk to the special education department and/or school psychologist
When in doubt, the teacher should privately discuss any concern regarding a student with a special education teacher or school psychologist first. That professional may be able to assist the teacher in determining whether it would be important to evaluate the child, or whether it would be important to contact the parent to ask questions, seek clarification, or point out a potential delay.

5. **Which of the following statements is NOT true about play?**

   A. Play helps develop motor skills
   B. Play starts off cooperative and becomes more solitary as children grow
   C. Play helps children learn about themselves and their interests
   D. Sports is an appropriate type of play for some, but not all, children

Answer: B. Play starts off cooperative and becomes more solitary as children grow
The stages of play development move from solitary (particularly in infancy stages) to cooperative (in early childhood), and while the emerging stages of cooperative play may be awkward (as children will at first not want to share toys, for example), with some guidance and experience children will learn how to be good peers and friends.

6. **Which of the following ways can a teacher implement to convey high expectations to students?**

   A. Communicate effectively with students and parents
   B. Dilute instruction to challenged students so they can experience success
   C. Speak to the students about your confidence in their ability to succeed
   D. Notify students of your expectations first and foremost

Answer: A. Dilute instruction to challenged students so they can experience success
Never lower standards or "dilute" instruction for certain students. It is the teacher's responsibility to ascertain the means to bring the student's academic performance up to standards.

7. Some examples of impediments students face when developing decision-making skills include:

    A. Inability to estimate negative consequences
    B. Succumbing to emotion over logic
    C. Inability to judge the reactions of their peers
    D. All of the above

Answer: D. All of the above
Cognitive, psychological, social, cultural, and even socioeconomic factors can all influence how young people approach decision-making, goal-setting, and being organized. All of these answers represent just some of the impediments students face when learning how to make decisions.

8. Research has shown that the organization of middle-level education is unique and important to adolescent learning because:

    A. It is a less personal environment than elementary school
    B. It engages in content area instruction
    C. The programs are not too exploratory
    D. Varied learning strategies accommodate curiosity and exploration

Answer: D. Varied learning strategies accommodate curiosity and exploration.
Middle-level education is designed to be a more personal environment for adolescents, as well as engage in significant amounts of interdisciplinary learning so as to enhance the relevance of material. In addition, varied learning strategies accommodate adolescent interests, curiosity and restlessness.

9. A positive _____ involves self-acceptance as a person, and does not imply feelings of superiority or perfection.

    A. self-image
    B. sense of confidence
    C. self-concept
    D. self-awareness

Answer: C. self concept.
A positive self-concept does not imply feelings of superiority, perfection, or competence/efficacy. Instead, a positive self-concept involves self-acceptance as a person and having a proper respect for oneself.

10. **Which of the following statements has been found to be true regarding students engaging in risky behaviors?**

   A. Engaging in risky behaviors often negatively impacts learning and development
   B. Anti-social behavior is a late sign that students are engaging in risky behavior.
   C. Adolescents' limited decision-making skills are not a factor relating to risky behaviors.
   D. Emotionally healthy students have a difficult time maintain control over their involvement in risky behaviors.

Answer: A. Engaging in risky behaviors often negatively impacts learning and development.
Researchers have shown that when students engage in risky behaviors it often negatively impacts their learning and development. Academically, students tend to start struggling and failing earlier, which further results in a lack of commitment to school.

11. **Which of the following statements does NOT demonstrate a teacher showing respect for the diversity of students in her classroom?**

   A. The teacher refrains from calling on reluctant students, forcing them to participate
   B. The teacher meets with students individually so as to learn about specifics such as the student's interests or to learn how the student likes to be addressed
   C. The teacher allows students to volunteer thoughts, opinions and ideas
   D. The teacher makes cultural connections that are relevant to instruction

Answer: A. The teacher refrains from calling on reluctant students, forcing them to participate
The teacher should allow the students to volunteer and then call on the more reluctant students to provide additional information or opinions. All opinions (which are not derogatory in case or by nature) are valid and should be reinforced as such by the teacher's approval.

12. **James has an assignment to interview an adult from another country. For his assignment, he is to conduct a short interview and view an authentic letter or journal of the adult. He is to compile everything into a wall display with information on the country as well. This assignment is an example of:**

   A. a Social Science unit
   B. inclusion
   C. establishing a culturally-rich environment
   D. an ELL assignment

Answer: C. establishing a culturally-rich environment
Teachers must create personalized learning communities where every student is a valued member and contributor of the classroom experiences. In classrooms where socio-cultural attributes of the student population are incorporated into the fabric of the learning process, dynamic interrelationships are created that enhance the learning experience and the personalization of learning.

13. Journals, reflections, exhibits, oral presentations, and portfolios are just some examples of _____.

    A. Cooperative learning
    B. Personalized learning communities
    C. Alternative assessments
    D. Differentiated instruction

Answer: C. Alternative assessments
Alternative assessment is an assessment where students create an answer or a response to a question or task, as opposed to traditional, inflexible assessments where students choose a prepared response from among a selection of responses, such as matching, multiple-choice or true/false.

14. Which of the following is NOT considered to be a difference in student learning ability?

    A. Giftedness
    B. Cerebral palsy
    C. Auditory processing disorder
    D. Dyslexia

Answer: A. Social developmental.
Dyslexia and attention, visual, and auditory processing disorders are just some disorders mentioned in the text that are likely affect a student's ability to learn. Cerebral palsy is considered a physical disorder.

15. When planning lessons and units for classroom instruction, teachers must target observable and measurable _____ in their lessons and units.

    A. objectives
    B. themes
    C. goals
    D. assessments

Answer: A. objectives.
As teachers plan from day to day, they need to be aware of their learning goals for their students, as well as their daily objectives within their lessons. Broadly, we can distinguish goals and objectives by suggesting that goals are long-term and often more abstract, immeasurable and vague. Objectives are short-term, specific, measurable, and must be clear.

16. **At the start of Mrs. McDonald's daily grammar lesson, she wrote "Students will learn to contrast adjectives and adverbs in written sentences" on the board for her students. This is an example of:**

    A. a clear objective
    B. an unclear objective
    C. a clear goal
    D. a unit introduction

Answer: A. a clear objective.
This is a clear objective. We know that the students should be able to get a sentence (age-appropriate length and complexity) and differentiate between adverbs and adjectives in a sentence; perhaps by possibly circling the words that are adjectives and underlining the words that are adverbs.

17. **When evaluating one's effectiveness as a teacher, it is important for the individual to:**

    A. reflect on their own teachings, as well as those of others, to determine if needs are being met.
    B. finish their education so they know how and what to teach
    C. teach their lessons over and over again
    D. come to terms with the fact that some students may never understand a specific concept.

Answer: A. reflect on their own teachings, as well as those of others, to determine if needs are being met.
The very nature of the teaching profession—the yearly cycle of doing the same thing over and over again—creates the tendency to fossilize, to quit growing, to end their own educational growth, and/or to become complacent. It is important for teachers to involve themselves in constant periods of reflection and self-reflection to ensure they are meeting the needs of the students.

18. **Which of the following describes a common issue with the sole use of textbooks for instruction?**

    A. Textbooks are suitable and age-appropriate
    B. Textbooks may reflect a single perspective or outdated societal values
    C. Textbooks provide detailed units with specific teaching procedures
    D. Textbooks follow the design and focus of the school administration

Answer: B. Textbooks may reflect a single perspective or outdated societal values
Most teachers choose to use textbooks, which are suitable to the age and developmental level of specific student populations. Textbooks reflect the values and assumptions of the society that produces them, while they also represent the knowledge and skills considered to be essential in becoming an educated adult. Textbooks, when used correctly, are a great aid and resource in the classroom so long as the teacher ensures the textbook appropriately represents current information as well as multiple perspectives.

19. According to the scope and sequences of most curriculum units/plans, _____ must be taken into consideration to determine quantifiably that student learning has taken place over the course of the unit.

    A. National and state standards
    B. learning objectives, goals, and assessments
    C. learning experiences
    D. All of the above

Answer: D. All of the above
All components of a lesson plan (including the unit description, learning targets, learning experiences, explanation of learning rationale and assessments) must be present to provide both quantifiable and qualitative data to ascertain whether student learning has taken place and whether effective teaching has occurred for the students. National and state learning standards must be taken into account because not only will the teacher and his students be measured by the students' scores at the end of the year, the school will also.

20. Taking attendance, gathering homework, "quiet study time", and assembling members for group work are all examples of _____.

    A. a typical elementary classroom morning
    B. unavoidable teacher "chores"
    C. nonproductive time
    D. All of the above

Answer: C. nonproductive time
Proper time management and allocation contribute to efficient classroom management and a positive learning environment. The items in the question are all examples or nonproductive events which are usually organizational and administrative tasks. Effective teachers prepare in advance as much as possible so as to avoid household chores in the classroom.

21. _____ deal(s) with the study of how to help the learner gain understanding about how knowledge is constructed, as well as how to consciously constructed knowledge.

    A. The metacognition learning theory
    B. Piaget's stages of development
    C. The brain-based learning theory
    D. The multiple intelligences theory

Answer: A. The metacognition learning theory
This is the definition of the metacognition learning theory. This cognitive approach to learning involves the teacher's understanding that teaching the student to process his/her own learning and mastery of skill provides the greatest learning and retention opportunities in the classroom. Students are taught to develop concepts and teach themselves skills in problem solving and critical thinking.

22. Mr. Sillars considers his students' social needs, as well as his curriculum, when designing and implementing his classroom management strategies. By doing so, he is utilizing the _____ learning theory to enhance student learning.

    A. brain-based
    B. cognitive
    C. constructivist
    D. behaviorism

Answer: D. behaviorism
Social and behavioral theories look at the social interactions of students in the classroom that instruct or impact learning opportunities in the classroom. Students are social beings that normally gravitate to action in the classroom, so teachers must be cognizant in planning classroom environments that provide both focus and engagement in maximizing learning opportunities.

23. Bloom's Taxonomy refers to:

    A. only higher-ordered thinking skills
    B. advanced communication skills
    C. multiple levels within the cognitive domain
    D. All of the above

Answer: C. multiple levels within the cognitive domain
Bloom's taxonomy references six skill levels within the cognitive domain: knowledge, comprehension, application, analysis, synthesis, and evaluation. Low order questions (recall, knowledge, define, analyze, etc.) are useful to begin the process. They insure the student is focused on the required information and understands what needs to be included in the thinking process. Higher-order thinking skills, often referred to as HOTS, refer to the top three levels of Bloom's Taxonomy: analysis, synthesis, and evaluation.

24. Which of the following statements is NOT true about effective questioning?

    A. Ask questions that require substantive answers
    B. Include questions with simple fact answers
    C. Don't confuse students with questions that pose contradictions to the topic
    D. Ask questions about current and real-life situations

Answer: B. Include questions with simple fact answers
Avoid questions where the answer is a simple fact or a one-word answer such as "What year was President Kennedy killed? It is better to have students expand on a question such as "What factors played into President Kennedy's assassination?"

25. Requiring students to keep assignment calendars helps students by teaching them to:

    A. keep materials organized in the classroom
    B. estimate the time needed for assignments and track due dates
    C. divide responsibilities amongst classmates and assignments
    D. practice leadership roles

Answer: B. estimate the time needed for assignments and track due dates
Teachers can help students by expecting that they keep calendars for themselves. In the calendars, they can write down homework assignments, estimate the amount of time they will need for certain assignments, and plug in important dates. They can also help students organize their learning environments by teaching them how to organize their own learning materials in folders.

26. Teaching students the use of _____ demonstrates an effective study skill that emphasizes the use of webs, maps and outlines to organize and relate material around a study topic.

    A. summarizing
    B. graphic organizers
    C. note-taking
    D. All of the above

Answer: B. graphic organizers
Using graphic organizers and concept web guides that center around a concept and the applications of the concept is an instructional strategy that teachers can use to guide students into further inquiry of the subject matter.

27. Socioeconomic status, family education, crisis factors, and stated teacher expectations are all examples of factors that:

    A. decrease achievement
    B. affect education
    C. increase learning
    D. Answers B and C

Answer: B. affect education
The student's capacity and potential for academic success within the overall educational experience are products of her or his total environment: classroom and school system; home and family; and neighborhood and community. All of these segments are interrelated and can be supportive, one of the other, or divisive, one against the other.

28. Which of the following terms describes the state of learning in which students and teachers focus on positive reinforcement, self-management, and monitoring of progress?

    A. Initial acquisition
    B. Advanced acquisition
    C. Maintenance
    D. Proficiency

Answer: D. Proficiency
As students progress through the states of learning, the teacher gradually decreases the amount of direct instruction and guidance and encourages the student to function independently. In the proficiency stage, teachers engage in positive reinforcement, progress monitoring, teaching of self-management, and increased expectations to progress learning. The emphasis here is to increase speed of performance to the automatic level with accuracy.

29. Megan's teacher has differentiated her art research project to include a section on demonstrating Impressionist brush techniques. By doing so, Megan's teacher has incorporated her _____ approach to learning in her assignment.

    A. Visual
    B. Auditory
    C. Kinesthetic
    D. Naturalistic

Answer: C. Kinesthetic
Kinesthetic learners learn by doing and experiencing so demonstrating an art technique would be an effective strategy for the student.

30. Mrs. Anderson engages her middle schoolers in peer review sessions, discussion journaling, and small-group learning. This classroom management style reflects Mrs. Anderson's knowledge that she:

    A. is aware of her students' developmental needs
    B. doesn't want to lecture all day long
    C. plans in-depth and complex activities for her class
    D. All of the above

Answer: A. is aware of her students' developmental needs
Middle and high school-level students have a tendency to socialize, and this can quickly allow the classroom situation to deteriorate, replacing the learning environment with chaos. In middle school, teachers can take advantage of this need to socialize to augment learning if planned well. Peer-reviews, "discussion" journaling, peer edits, pair and small-group learning all work well at this level as students are ready to work with others and will do so in such a positive environment.

31. **In order to establish a classroom that encourages collaborative, respectful and supportive interactions among students, teachers must NOT:**

    A. encourage the extensive participation from all students
    B. model how to welcome and consider all points of view
    C. positively affirm all student ideas
    D. deter ideas that are amiss from the topic

Answer: D. deter ideas that are amiss from the topic
Even if somewhat amiss, the teacher should receive the idea while perhaps offering a modification or corrected statement (for more factual pieces of information). The idea is for students to feel confident and safe in being able to express their thoughts or ideas. Only then will students be able to engage in independent discussions that consider and respect everyone's statements.

32. **Which of the following statements is NOT an important strategy when it comes to running an organized classroom geared for optimal learning?**

    A. Having prepared and ample materials for each lesson
    B. Allowing students to return materials poorly
    C. Having in-place procedures for distributing materials
    D. Having classroom management policies in place

Answer: B. Allowing students to return materials poorly
Students should be taught to replace the materials in the proper places to obtain them easily for the next time they are used. At higher grade levels, the teacher is concerned with materials such as textbooks, written instructional aides, worksheets, computer programs, etc., which must be produced, maintained, distributed, and collected for future use.

33. **Mrs. Doyle is a new teacher who has realized it is taking a long time to get her class situated in the morning. Which of the following strategies would help her save time?**

    A. Calling out roll each morning while marking present and absent students
    B. Searching through all materials each morning before starting each activity
    C. Having each student come up to show completed homework assignments each class
    D. Laminating a class seating chart to mark empty desks for roll and to reuse each day

Answer: D. Laminating a class seating chart to mark empty desks for roll and to reuse each day
A teacher can spot absentees in seconds by noting the empty seats, rather than calling each student's name which could take as long as five minutes. Laminating the chart allows the teacher to make daily notes right on the chart. The teacher may also efficiently keep track of who is volunteering and who is answering questions.

34. **Which of the following statements describes the small group socialization entitled "trading cards"?**

    A. Children build towers with a deck of card, working together
    B. Children share information about themselves on self-made trading cards
    C. Children move math cards to "find" the right answer in a timed activity
    D. Children create small-group stories to laminate on cards

Answer: B. Children share information about themselves on self-made trading cards
In the game Trading Cards, children can share information about themselves by creating personalized trading cards. This could be used as an "ice-breaker" activity. Answer A refers to an example of "Can You Build It"; Answer C refers to an example of a "Mad Minute Relay"; and Answer D refers to a small-group authoring activity.

35. **Which of the following terms describes the element of cooperative learning that states that all team members' unique contributions are required for success?**

    A. Small group skills
    B. Positive Interdependence
    C. Face-to-Face Interaction
    D. Group Processing

Answer: B. Positive Interdependence
According to positive interdependence, one of the five elements of cooperative learning, all members' efforts are required for success. The group can't succeed without the each individual's unique contribution. Each member is indispensable for success.

36. **Which of the following is NOT a common critique of block or modular scheduling?**

    A. Long instructional blocks are difficult for younger or less mature children
    B. Students can be negatively affected much if they miss a day of school
    C. Teachers are always able to plan what they want to cover in the large block
    D. It is difficult for teachers to cover ample material in advanced classes

Answer: C. Teachers are always able to plan what they want to cover in the large block
Poor planning could result in not enough material for the longer time block, and over the course of a year, this could result in a lot of lost instructional time

37. Using the available _____ to perform administrative tasks is increasingly becoming a necessity for the modern teacher.

    A. technology
    B. curriculum
    C. standards
    D. materials

Answer: A. technology
As new educational programs, services and techniques are continually introduced, demands upon the teacher's time (in and out of the classroom) are increased. The technology itself will continue to change and, presumably, improve the processes we use to access and manipulate a variety of functional tools for the classroom and for administrative use, and the teacher should stay informed about these changes and the availability to access new or enhanced technologies through his or her school system.

38. Volunteers, when used appropriately, can enhance a classroom setting by:

    A. offering assistance to just a few students
    B. relieving the teacher of some teaching responsibility
    C. providing individualized attention to students
    D. helping to plan lessons and activities

Answer: C. providing individualized attention to students
Volunteers can provide extra individualized attention to students while the rest of the class is engaged in other work, or they can offer additional assistance in small group activities.

39. This behavior management technique refers to the concept that a preferred behavior that frequently occurs can be used to increase a less preferred behavior with a low rate of occurrence.

    A. token economy
    B. contingency contract
    C. prompting
    D. modeling

Answer: B. contingency contract
Also known as the Premack Principle or "Grandma's Law", contingency contracting is based on the concept that a preferred behavior that frequently occurs can be used to increase a less preferred behavior with a low rate of occurrence. Contingencies can also be simple verbal contracts, such as the teacher telling a child that he or she may earn a treat or special activity for completion of a specific academic activity.

40. **Common examples that would BEST describe the age-appropriate and high behavior expectations in an upper elementary or middle school classroom include:**

    A. raising your hand to speak; not physical or verbal disruptions; and speaking and behaving in an age-appropriate manner
    B. keeping hands to oneself; show respect to others; and listen carefully
    C. no cheating or plagiarizing; no obscene language; no inappropriate displays of affection; and no electronic devices in the classroom
    D. clean up your area; share with others; and take turns with classmates

Answer: A. raising your hand to speak; not physical or verbal disruptions; and speaking and behaving in an age-appropriate manner
Answer A best fits the expectations of a common middle school classroom. Answer B and D are more the general expectations of a young elementary of early childhood classroom, while Answer C includes examples of common high school expectations.

41. **What is the estimated number of rules a classroom teacher should create with her students and display in the classroom?**

    A. 1-2
    B. 2-3
    C. 4-6
    D. 7-8

Answer: C. 4-6
About four to six classroom rules should be posted where students can easily see and read them. These rules should be stated positively, and describe specific behaviors so they are easy to understand. When the teacher clarifies and models the expected behavior for the students, she is stating the behavior that is expected from students in the classroom.

42. **Robert, an 11-yr-old is Mrs. Robbins' fifth grade class, is repeatedly leaving his seat during his teacher's lessons. Which of the following strategies is NOT recommended in helping Robert to modify his negative behavior?**

    A. making a clear and concise statement about expected behavior
    B. making a harsh and loud statement to get a point across
    C. referring to the posted classroom rules
    D. swiftly addressing Robert's disregard for the rules as soon as he leaves his seat or even as early as when the teacher sees him begin to stand

Answer: B. making a harsh and loud statement to get a point across
Verbal techniques, which may be effective in modifying student behavior and setting the classroom tone, include simply stating the student's name, explaining briefly and succinctly what the student is doing that is inappropriate and what the student should be doing. The teacher must be careful to control the voice, both the volume and the tone. Research indicates that soft reprimands are more effective in controlling disruptive behavior than loud reprimands and that when soft reprimands are used fewer are needed.

43. **Much valuable information occurs in communications which occur between teacher and student. Which of the following is a significant factor that teachers must consider when assessing student learning?**

    A. A noisy air conditioner
    B. A learning disability
    C. Level of required teacher assistance
    D. All of the above

Answer: D. All of the above
While teachers should never consider that all student learning is based on teachers communicating to students, much valuable information does occur in the transmission of words between teacher and student. Learning preference, learning abilities and even the environment of a classroom (a noisy AC unit that impacts students' ability to hear) all can affect learning.

44. **Mrs. Allen is conducting a discussion on the three types of rock with her fifth grade science class. As she asks the students to provide an example of an igneous rock, Jason raises his hand to go to the rest room. Mrs. Allen nods yes while repeating her question. What is this an example of?**

    A. redirecting the discussion to maintain learning flow
    B. an insincere response
    C. an unavoidable class disruption
    D. a housekeeping task

Answer: A. redirecting the discussion to maintain learning flow
The focus of the classroom discussion should be on the subject matter and controlled by teacher-posed questions. However, when the student response is incorrect or off-task, this task is a little more difficult. The teacher must redirect the discussion to the task at hand, and at the same time not devalue the student response. It is more difficult for the teacher to avoid digression when a student poses a non-academic question.

45. **Some teachers choose not to simply correct their students during a discussion. Instead, they choose methods, such as discussing or amplifying the response, in order to _____.**

    A. waste classroom time by repeating the answers
    B. isolate students in the discussion
    C. provide no feedback
    D. show that student responses are accepted and valuable

Answer: D. show that student responses are accepted and valuable
Teachers show more acceptance and value to student responses, not by correcting, but by acknowledging, amplifying, discussing or restating the comment or question. If you allow a student response, even if it is blurted out, you must acknowledge the student response and tell the student the quality of the response.

46. Inductive reasoning:

  A. draws conclusions from finite examples
  B. considers simple facts or statements to arrive at more general conclusion
  C. theories based on assumed observations that contain at least one prediction
  D. arrives at an explanatory hypothesis

Answer: B. observe student reactions to the question as a clue to their understanding
Generally speaking, complex concepts can be taught in two manners: deductively or inductively. In an inductive manner, the students will derive the definition from examples and non-examples provided by the teacher. The students will test these examples and non-examples to ascertain if they possess the attributes that meet the criteria of the definition.

47. Brainstorming, discussions, problem solving, dramatizations, and learning centers are all good examples of:

  A. varying instructional strategies
  B. higher-ordered thinking skills
  C. inquiry
  D. cooperative learning

Answer: A. varying instructional strategies
Classrooms have begun to drift away from being entirely composed of lectures (or direct instruction). By varying presentation of material, teachers increase learning in their classrooms. There are literally hundreds of instructional techniques that can be used at many levels from early childhood through advanced high school courses. The strategies listed in the question above are just a few ways to vary instruction.

48. Why are teacher observations critical to the structure, pacing and effectiveness of a lesson?

  A. teachers are able to assess the needs of the students
  B. observations help to drive the lesson
  C. teachers can adjust instructional strategies as needed
  D. All of the above

Answer: D. All of the above
The value of teacher observations cannot be underestimated. It is through the use of observations that the teacher is able to informally assess the needs of the students during instruction. These observations will drive the lesson and determine the direction that the lesson will take based on student activity and behavior.

49. **Which of the following strategies is NOT a method teachers can use to increase motivation in their classrooms?**

    A. Ask thought-provoking questions
    B. Find connections between material and student experiences
    C. Utilize charts, games or manipulatives to explore topics
    D. Use direct instruction to increase recall and boost confidence

Answer: D. Use direct instruction to increase recall and boost confidence
Educators are finding, however, that if students are motivated to learn, they will invest more effort in participation and classroom assignments if they feel there is a purpose to the work, and answers A, B, and C are all methods used to increase motivation.

50. **When evaluating learning materials for a classroom, which of the following questions is LEAST important in that consideration?**

    A. Will this material promote retention?
    B. Will this subject interest my students?
    C. Does this material promote interdisciplinary learning?
    D. Are these activities hands on?

Answer: A. Will this material promote retention?
Answers B, C, and D (and more listed in Skill 8.5) should all be considered as a teacher evaluates materials from not only her perspective, but the perspective of her students. A better question to ask, rather than question A, would be "Does this material promote critical thinking?"

51. **_____ motivation is motivation that comes from the expectation of rewards or punishments.**

    A. Intrinsic
    B. Fear
    C. Extrinsic
    D. Self-

Answer: C. Extrinsic
Extrinsic motivation is motivation that comes from the expectation of rewards or punishments. The rewards and punishments can be varied.

52. **What is a downfall in using punishment (or the aim to avoid such punishment) as a motivator?**

    A. Students become viewed as unfair and unorganized
    B. Students eventually do not fear the teacher anymore
    C. Students become too consumed with fear they can't focus on learning
    D. Students fail to retain information as well.

Answer: C. Students become more consumed with fear they can't focus on learning
If punishment is *always* used as a motivator, students may be more consumed with fear than with the frame of mind that is most conducive to learning. Punishments, if they are reasonable and if students know what to expect (with consistent application), can be useful in making sure students behave appropriately.

53. **When considering student motivation, learning and on-task behavior, research suggests teamwork and cooperative learning activities _____ student behavior problems.**

    A. increase
    B. decrease
    C. don't affect
    D. eliminate

Answer: B. decrease
Research substantiates that teamwork and/or cooperative group projects decrease student behavior problems and increase student on-task behavior. Students who are directly involved with learning activities are more motivated to complete a task to the best of their ability.

54. **Having students create daily lists and/or unit goals is a strategy that helps to:**

    A. create seatwork for students
    B. assess daily learning
    C. increase student motivation
    D. All of the above

Answer: C. increase student motivation
One strategy to increase student motivation is to have students create daily and unit lists or goals for learning. Stating these goals increases student focus and lets them see their daily progress and accomplishments.

55. Many school computers have strict space limitations, so when teachers can not store files on the hard drive, another option is to store large files on portable or external _____, such as a flash drive.

   A. storage devices
   B. wiring systems
   C. computers
   D. Answers A and B

Answer: A. storage devices
The amount of storage space on a hard drive has become increasingly important. Storage devices enable computers to save documents and other important files for future editing. An option that adds portability for students to move small files from one computer to another is a flash drive.

56. Which of the following is the likely type of network to be found in a school building?

   A. wide-area network
   B. local-area network
   C. campus-area network
   D. home-area network

Answer: B. local-area network
In a local-area network, the computers are all contained within the same building, such as a school. Wide-area networks are connected through telephones or radio waves; campus-area network are connected within a school campus or military base; and home-area networks are connected within a private home.

57. What is the suggested consequence for a student who abuses or violates any parts of his or her district's computer usage agreement?

   A. three days detention
   B. provide student and his or her parent with a written warning
   C. have all access to school computers or educational technology blocked
   D. have an aid supervise the student's computer usage

Answer: C. have all access to school computers or educational technology blocked
Internet usage agreements define a number of criteria of technology use that a students must agree to in order to have access to school computers. Students who violate any parts of the computer usage agreement are subject to have all access to school computers or other educational technology blocked, which, for the student needing to print a paper using the school computer and printer, could make the difference in handing assignments in on time or receiving a lower grade for late assignments.

58. Of what important fact should teachers make older students aware prior to students' usage of Internet resources for a school assignment?

A. accurate information is hard to find on the Internet
B. material on the Internet may or may not have been approved for accurate content before publication
C. only pre-selected sites can be used
D. it is impossible to verify validity on Internet sites

Answer: B. material on the Internet may or may not have been approved for accurate content before publication
Unlike newspapers and books that undergo a fact checker or editor, the Internet is an open forum for web site, blogs, posts, opinions and information. Students must first be made aware of this fact alone (that material posted on the Internet may or may not have been approved for content before it was available to all. Then, students will need to evaluate the material for accuracy, validity and if it suits his or her needs.

59. Which of the following is NOT a primary category of how technological tools can be used in a school?

A. instructional/practice/assessment
B. classroom management
C. research
D. creation

Answer: B. material on the Internet may or may not have been approved for accurate content before publication
Instructional technology tools can be divided into three primary categories: instruction/practice/assessment, creation, and research. Technological tools are varied, and to ensure that the ones selected for use in the classroom are effective at providing students with good instruction, teachers will want to think about the relationship between instructional objectives and the technological tools.

60. This category of technological instructional tools refers to where students use word processing, spreadsheets, graphic, or multi-media tools to demonstrate proficiency with both the lesson knowledge and the technology.

A. instructional/practice/assessment
B. classroom management
C. research
D. creation

Answer: D. creation
Creation, a category of instructional tools, refers to activities where students use word processing tools, spreadsheet tools, graphic tools, or multi-media tools to either demonstrate proficiency with the technology, or more likely, to demonstrate (or practice) proficiency with a skill that can be evidenced through technology.

61. **Mr. Jacobs utilizes a web page to list his class assignments, homework, upcoming tests and other relevant important dates. What is one or Mr. Jacobs' reasons for presenting information about his class work online?**

    A. more easily communicate with parents
    B. presents his class work in a professional and organized manner
    C. gain professional respect from parents, colleagues and administrators
    D. All of the above

Answer: D. All of the above
In general, we know that the more a teacher communicates with parents, the more likely parents will trust the teacher and assist the teacher in his or her methods and strategies. And parents are impressed by teachers who take the time to put together something in a professional manner. So, teachers will earn much more respect from families by providing information in a timely and professional manner.

62. **What is one benefit from allowing students to collaborate when working on computer programs in the classroom?**

    A. more easily communicate with parents
    B. students can work with their friends to get their work completed
    C. collaboration on computers will help student engage in a more productive, help-centered learning environment
    D. All of the above

Answer: D. All of the above
As technological tools are complicated and complex, pair and small group work better facilitates stronger, social-based learning. Remember, social opportunities to learn technology will help students to engage in a more productive, friendly, and help-centered fashion. Learning together, particularly in technology, can indeed reduce any anxiety or fear a student may have.

63. **When a teacher asks student to produce a technological product, the teacher must consider several elements in their final product. When the teacher considers the *relevance* of a final product, he or she is considering:**

    A. the method of technology used
    B. to whom the product is directed and what is needed to be comprehended
    C. how the product was used to prove proficiency of the content
    D. the format of the piece

Answer: C. how the product was used to prove proficiency of the content
Relevance could actually be the most important element. Students may demonstrate incredible proficiency with the technological tool, but if they do not demonstrate how it was used to prove proficiency on the content, then the activity was done for the sake of the technological tool only.

64. This kind of assessment is a structured, infrequent measure of learner achievement.

    A. Journal
    B. Informal
    C. Formal
    D. Observation

Answer: C. Formal
Formal assessment is a structured infrequent measure of learner achievement. It involves the use of test and exam. Exams are used to measure the learner's progress.

65. Multiple choice tests are an example of:

    A. Subjective assessment
    B. Objective assessment
    C. Informal assessment
    D. Authentic assessment

Answer: B. Objective assessment
Most objective tests will include multiple-choice questions, matching and true/false questions that include a selection of answer choices. The correct answer can be found using a simple process of elimination of decoy or incomplete answers.

66. What is one disadvantage to formal assessment?

    A. Multiple-choice tests are too easy
    B. These assessments don't always measure specific retention
    C. These assessments don't always measure achievement
    D. These assessments don't always provide a complete picture of a student's ability

Answer: D. These assessments don't always provide a complete picture of a student's ability
Formal assessments do not always provide a full picture of a student's capabilities. They tend have multiple choice questions and/or some written format, and they rarely challenge the student to originate their own answer, showing their depth of understanding. Teachers must keep in mind that formal assessment is one component of assessment, and must be combined with other types of assessment for a more accurate representation of students' abilities.

67. **Mrs. O'Neill is recording through codes the performance of her students while reading aloud. This coding is an example of an informal assessment called a(n):**

    A. observation
    B. running record
    C. journal
    D. essay

Answer: B. running record
A simple-to-administer, information-rich evaluation of a child's reading strengths and weaknesses is the running reading record. The teacher uses a simple coding system to record what a child does while reading text out loud. At a later time the teacher can go back to the record and assess what the child knows about reading and what the teacher needs to address in an effort to help the student become a better reader.

68. **Researchers suggest that a benefit of a true/false test item is:**

    A. susceptibility to guessing
    B. the questions are difficult to construct
    C. there are limited learning outcomes it can measure
    D. is useful in identifying cause and effect relationships

Answer: D. is useful in identifying cause and effect relationships
Another common form of objective question is the true/false test item. Gronlund and Linn point out some limitations to this test item is its susceptibility to guessing, the difficulty involved in constructing a true/false item that is valid, and the limited specific learning outcomes it can measure. However, they also point out its usefulness in identifying cause and effect relationships as well as distinguishing fact and opinion.

69. **Mr. Rockford is mentoring a new teacher, Mr. Harsche. Mr. Rockford has noticed that Mr. Harsche's comments on the students' English essays are too vague with comments such as "Work on grammar." Which of the following comments could Mr. Rockford suggest to Mr. Harsche in order for him to better provide more useful feedback to his students?**

    A. "This should be clearer."
    B. "Review last week's grammar lesson to improve."
    C. "See me."
    D. "Be sure to always use a comma to separate independent clauses in the same sentence."

Answer: D. "Be sure to always use a comma to separate independent clauses in the same sentence."
Specific feedback is particularly important. Comments like, "This should be clearer" and "Your grammar needs to be worked on" provide information that students may already know. They may already know they have a problem with clarity. What they can benefit from is commentary that provides very specific actions students could take to make something more clearly or to improve his or her grammar.

70. Benjamin is a student in Mr. Turner's American History class. He has asked a question that is slightly off topic from the lesson, but initiated by the lesson content, and it has sparked the interest of his classmates. What is the ideal thing for Mr. Turner to do at that moment in class?

    A. have Benjamin conduct independent research on the topic
    B. move forward and ignore the question
    C. respond to this "teachable moment" and adjust the class discussion
    D. re-teach the original concept so as to get the class back on task

Answer: C. respond to this "teachable moment" and adjust the class discussion
It is important that teachers pay close attention for things that might increase optimal learning. That teacher would be irresponsible to just move forward and ignore the question. To ignore it would be to say to students that learning is supposed to be boring and that school is not supposed to feed the intellectual interests of students. Assessing a sense of curiosity in the students, the teacher engages students in a brief answer to the question.

71. What is one benefit of a teacher using an online web site or classroom management system?

    A. Attendance can be tracked
    B. Class assignments, tests and due dates can be viewed anytime
    C. Parents can communicate almost directly with the teacher at their convenience
    D. All of the above

Answer: D. All of the above
Some teachers maintain classroom web sites that list a class calendar, and sometimes even test dates, project due dates and other helpful information. Other teachers utilize online classroom management systems where attendance, grades, notes, assignments, class calendars and more are all available in one place through a login.

72. Mrs. Gains wishes to better communicate with her students' parents on a more regular basis. What is a strategy Mrs. Gains can implement in order to achieve improved communication?

    A. Create a class newsletter
    B. Call home regarding negative behavior
    C. Send a note home once a year
    D. Meeting at conferences is sufficient

Answer: A. Create a class newsletter
Parents love to know what is going on in the classroom, and newsletters help them feel included. In newsletters, teachers can provide suggestions on how parents can help with the educational goals of the school. Parents often equate phone calls from teachers with news about misbehaviors of their children. Teachers can change that tone by calling parents with good news. Or they can send frequent, positive notes home with students.

73. **Three of the following four statements suggest ways for teachers to work with diverse groups in the classroom. Which statement is NOT a suggested way to encourage positivity in diverse classrooms?**

    A. show respect to all parents, students and families
    B. disregard negative actions from difficult families
    C. talk personally with each student
    D. emphasize partnerships with students to enhance their education and development

Answer: B. disregard negative actions from difficult families
Teachers will need to be patient with difficult families, realizing that certain methods of criticism (including verbal attacks, etc.) are unacceptable. Such circumstances would require the teacher to get assistance from an administrator. This situation, however, is very unusual, and most teachers will find that when they really attempt to be friendly and personal with parents, the parents will reciprocate and assist in the educational program.

74. **Which of the following is NOT a purpose of a parent-teacher conference?**

    A. to obtain information about the child
    B. share information with the parents about the performance and behavior of the child
    C. socialize with the teacher to catch up on school events
    D. request parental support or involvement in specific activities

Answer: C. socialize with the teacher to catch up on school events
A parent-teacher conference is not the ideal time to socialize with a child's teacher. Most time, you as the teacher will have a limited amount of time (typically 10-15 minutes) to share the positive aspects of a child's performance and learning, as well as any concerns you have. Then the parents will need to express questions or concerns. It is better to refrain from socializing here and save that for another time such as a social school event.

75. **_____can supplement the minimized and marginal educational resources of school communities.**

    A. Advanced curriculum materials
    B. Community resources
    C. Parents
    D. Administrators

Answer: B. Community resources
With state and federal educational funding becoming increasingly subject to legislative budget cuts, school communities welcome the financial support that community resources can provide in terms of discounted prices on high end supplies (e.g. computers, printers, and technology supplies), along with providing free notebooks, backpacks and student supplies for low income students who may have difficulty obtaining the basic supplies for school.

76. **According to some researchers, connections between the school and the community encourage:**

    A. a commitment to volunteering
    B. a sense of community and value
    C. greater retention rates of graduating students
    D. All of the above

Answer: D. All of the above
The bridge to effective learning for students begins with a collaborative approach by all stakeholders that support the educational needs of students. Underestimating the power and integral role of the community institutions in impacting the current and future goals of students can carry high stakes for students beyond the high school years who are competing for college access, student internships, and entry level jobs in the community. When community institutions provide students and teachers with meaningful connections and input, the commitment is apparent in terms of volunteering, loyalty and professional promotion.

77. **Team teaching consists of:**

    A. mentoring systems
    B. two or more teachers involved in the same classroom instruction
    C. one grade level of teachers integrating subjects across the grade and then teaching one of those subjects to all grade classes
    D. groups of educators of the same discipline (but for different levels) working to plan curriculum

Answer: B. two or more teachers involved in the same classroom instruction
Team teaching consists of two or more teachers involved in the classroom instruction. In this system, teachers share the roles of instructor, monitor, and additional supporter, etc. to share the instructional workload and increase individual student achievement.

78. **This educational professional serves as the leader in the development and implementation of a subject.**

    A. technology coordinator
    B. child study team
    C. curriculum coordinator
    D. subject administrator

Answer: C. curriculum coordinator
Curriculum coordinators serve as the leader in the development and implementation of a subject. These professionals work with teachers who are involved in instruction of a particular subject.

79. **How can teachers utilize resources outside the school to enhance professional development?**

    A. research and make use of state initiatives
    B. utilize training and workshops provided by service centers
    C. work with universities to test new strategies and activities
    D. All of the above

Answer: D. All of the above
Outside of the school, service centers provide professional development opportunities. Also, state initiatives often provide unique ways of approaching common educational problems. For example, many schools get extra funding for reading programs, community service learning programs, and math programs. Finally, teachers can get involved with universities which are hoping to test new strategies and activities with students. While teachers learn new techniques, the universities get terrific data.

80. **What is the typical first step for a principal conducting a teacher appraisal to take?**

    A. evaluate and establish the goals and objectives teachers will work to attain
    B. provide recommendations for professional development
    C. encourage the teacher to seek out support from other teachers and/or mentor
    D. alleviate the teacher's concern

Answer: A. evaluate and establish the goals and objectives teachers will work to attain
A teacher appraisal is merely a method of "assessing" a teacher and providing them with feedback to help them improve practice. Usually, the process begins with principals working on particular goals and objectives that teachers will work to attain throughout the year. These goals and objectives typically are the things that principals will look to see improvement on within the school year.

81. **Which of the following is a constructive outcome of teacher self-assessment and self-reflection?**

    A. the teacher can identify what areas they should not teach
    B. the teacher can contribute information to academic trends
    C. the teacher realizes which upcoming staff development opportunities are futile
    D. the teacher comes to identify areas of skill that require improvement

Answer: D. the teacher comes to identify areas of skill that require improvement
When a teacher is involved in the process of self-reflection and self-assessment, one of the common outcomes is that the teacher comes to identify areas of skill or knowledge that require more research or improvement on her part. She may become interested in overcoming a particular weakness in her performance or may decide to attend a workshop or consult with a mentor to learn more about a particular area of concern.

82. Which of the following educational professionals is NOT typically part of a Child Study/Core Team?

    A. special education teacher
    B. school psychologist
    C. guidance counselor
    D. curriculum coordinator

Answer: D. curriculum coordinator
Many schools have a committee designated for addressing these needs such as a Child Study Team or Core Team. These teams are made up of both regular and exceptional education teachers, school psychologists, guidance counselors, and administrators. The particular student's classroom teacher usually has to complete some initial paper work and will need to do some behavioral observations.

83. Mr. Jackral suspects Jeremy, one his students, is being physically abused. What should be Mr. Jackral's initial step?

    A. wait to affirm the abuse
    B. talk to the student's parents
    C. talk to administration immediately
    D. talk to a colleague and think it over before acting

Answer: C. talk to administration immediately
There is no time given as an acceptable or safe period of time to wait before reporting, so hesitation to report may be a cause for action against you. Do not wait once your suspicion is firm. All you need to have is a reasonable suspicion, not actual proof, which is the job for the investigators. It is the duty of any citizen who suspects abuse and neglect to make a report to their administrator/child protective services (an organization which identifies and handles cases of abuse), and it is especially important and required for State licensed and certified persons to make a report.

84. Ms. Allen, the school Media Specialist, has seen a new teacher, Ms. Bellamy copying a chapter of a children's literature novel for use in her classroom. Should Ms. Allen approach Ms. Bellamy to discuss copyright infringement according to the "Guidelines for Classroom Copying in Nonprofit Educational Institutions"?

    A. yes; a chapter of prose exceeds the guidelines
    B. no; no copyright infringement has occurred
    C. no; a chapter of prose is acceptable by the guidelines
    D. yes; no copying of books is allowed

Answer: A. yes; a chapter of prose exceeds the guidelines
Many print instructional materials carry statements that allow production of multiple copies for classroom use, provided they adhere to the "Guidelines for Classroom Copying in Nonprofit Educational Institutions." Teachers may duplicate enough copies to provide one per student per course, provided that they meet the tests of brevity, spontaneity, and cumulative effect. However, an entire chapter of prose exceeds the guidelines of "excerpts less than 1000 words".

85. **A common pressure for new teachers is:**

    A. the intense rules and regulations regarding behavioral management and professionalism
    B. likelihood of abuse violations
    C. maintaining a toolkit of instructional strategies
    D. All of the above

Answer: A. the intense rules and regulations regarding behavioral management and professionalism
Teachers are under intense rules and regulations to maintain the highest degree of conduct and professionalism in the classroom. It is imperative that teachers educating today's young people have the highest regard for professionalism and be proper role models for students in and out of the classrooms.

86. **Which of the following pieces of information is NOT required to be compiled in a student's permanent file?**

    A. medical and physical information
    B. educational assessments, attendance and anecdotes
    C. social interests
    D. personal information

Answer: C. social interests
Social interests may be listed by default, but they are not required. Pertinent individual information contained in the permanent record includes the student's attendance, grade averages, and schools attended. Personal information such as parents' names and addresses, immunization records, child's height and weight, and narrative information about the child's progress and physical and mental well being is an important aspect of the permanent record.

87. **The contents of a students' permanent record:**

    A. should be indicative of student aptitude
    B. are highly confidential
    C. should be constructive and presented positively
    D. All of the above

Answer: D. All of the above
The contents of any student records should be indicative of the student's academic aptitude and/or achievement. The information contained should never be in any way derogatory or potentially damaging. It is important to keep in mind that others who view the contents of the records may form an opinion of the student based on the information in the student's record or file.

88. Reliability of an academic assessment refers to:

   A. the extent that assessments are consistent over time and setting
   B. the appropriateness of the test scores
   C. the ease of the procedures of the test
   D. the accessibility of academic information on the test

Answer: A. the extent that assessments are consistent over time and setting
Reliability refers to the extent that assessments are consistent over time and setting. This essentially means that an assessment given at different times of day, on different days, in different classrooms, and by different administrators should all yield the same result.

89. Some of the primary responsibilities of _____ include monitoring operations of schools, hiring teachers, managing bus and food services.

   A. a school district
   B. a local state service center
   C. a state government
   D. the US Department of Education

Answer: A. a school district
Districts are set up to run the day-to-day operations of schools. They deal with the hiring of teachers, the management of bus and food services, the facilities of schools, and many more things. Under the districts are the schools. So while a teacher may work at a particular school, the teacher is really an employee of the district.

90. It is crucial that teacher maintain the highest of professional standards. In order to do so, teachers must:

   A. collaborate with peers professionally
   B. continue their own professional development with higher education and professional organizations
   C. utilize state and community resources
   D. All of the above

Answer: D. All of the above
Teachers must maintain the highest professional standards for themselves. To do so, teachers must utilize the practices of this book and their state's educational resources, including professional development, collaboration with peers, continuing higher education, professional organizations, community resources and other resources to stay current in the profession of teaching. It is through these resources that teachers become, and remain, knowledgeable enough to be effective advocates for their students and their profession.

Answer Key

1.	D	31.	D	61.	D
2.	D	32.	B	62.	D
3.	C	33.	D	63.	C
4.	D	34.	B	64.	C
5.	B	35.	B	65.	B
6.	A	36.	C	66.	D
7.	D	37.	A	67.	B
8.	D	38.	C	68.	D
9.	C	39.	B	69.	D
10.	A	40.	A	70.	C
11.	A	41.	C	71.	D
12.	C	42.	B	72.	A
13.	C	43.	D	73.	B
14.	A	44.	A	74.	C
15.	A	45.	D	75.	B
16.	A	46.	B	76.	D
17.	A	47.	A	77.	B
18.	B	48.	D	78.	C
19.	D	49.	D	79.	D
20.	C	50.	A	80.	A
21.	A	51.	C	81.	D
22.	D	52.	C	82.	D
23.	C	53.	B	83.	C
24.	B	54.	C	84.	A
25.	B	55.	A	85.	A
26.	B	56.	B	86.	C
27.	B	57.	C	87.	D
28.	D	58.	B	88.	A
29.	C	59.	B	89.	A
30.	A	60.	D	90.	D

www.ingramcontent.com/pod-product-compliance
Lightning Source LLC
LaVergne TN
LVHW061319060426
835507LV00019B/2220